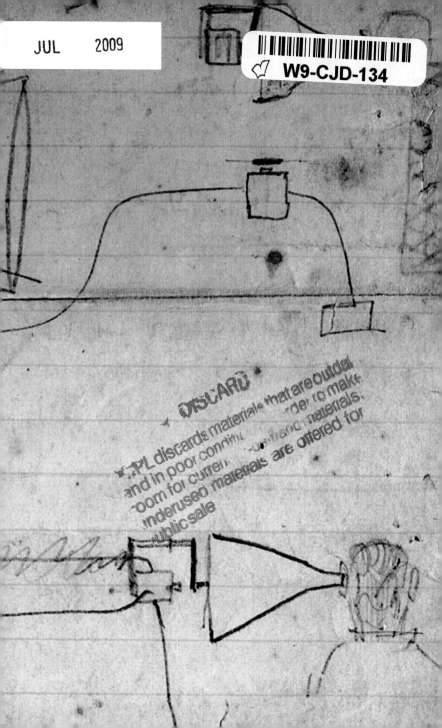

JUL 2009

W9-CJD-134

Alexander Graham Bell Invents

Alexander Graham Bell
Invents

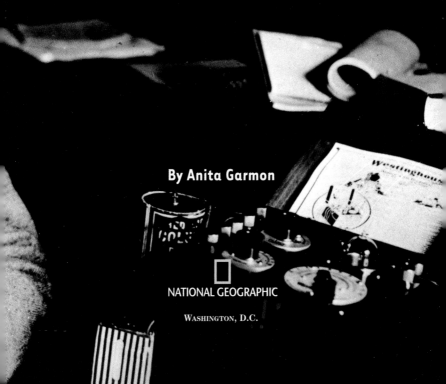

By Anita Garmon

NATIONAL GEOGRAPHIC

WASHINGTON, D.C.

Founded in 1888, the National Geographic Society is one of the largest nonprofit scientific and educational organizations in the world. It reaches more than 285 million people worldwide each month through its official journal, NATIONAL GEOGRAPHIC, and its four other magazines; the National Geographic Channel; television documentaries; radio programs; films; books; videos and DVDs; maps; and interactive media. National Geographic has funded more than 8,000 scientific research projects and supports an education program combating geographic illiteracy.

For more information, please call
1-800-NGS-LINE (647-5463) or write to the following address:

National Geographic Society
1145 17th Street N.W.
Washington, D.C. 20036-4688
U.S.A.

Visit us online at www.nationalgeographic.com/books

For information about special discounts for bulk purchases, please contact
National Geographic Books Special Sales at ngspecsales@ngs.org

For rights or permissions inquiries, please contact National Geographic
Books Subisidiary Rights: ngbookrights@ngs.org

Library of Congress Cataloging-in-Publication Data

Garmon, Anita.
  Alexander Graham Bell invents / by Anita Garmon.
       p. cm. -- (National Geographic history chapters)
  ISBN 978-1-4263-0189-6 (library)
1. Bell, Alexander Graham, 1847-1922--Juvenile literature.   2. Inventors--United States--Biography--Juvenile literature.   3. Telephone--United States--History--Juvenile literature.   I. Title.
TK6143.B4G37 2007
621.385092--dc22

                         2007007828

Photo Credits
Front Cover: © Stock Montage/Getty Images; Spine, Endpaper, 10, 12, 16, 19, 21, 32-33, 34: © Library of Congress; 2-3: Snark/Art Resource; 6, 11, 22: © Bettmann/CORBIS; 8, 13, 14, 18: © Bell Family/NGS Image Collection; 20: © Time Life Pictures/Getty Images; 23: © National Archives and Records Administration; 24: © Bridgeman Art Library, NY; 26, 30, 35: © The Granger Collection, NY; 28-29: © Getty Images.

Endsheets: A sketch drawn by Alexander Graham Bell.

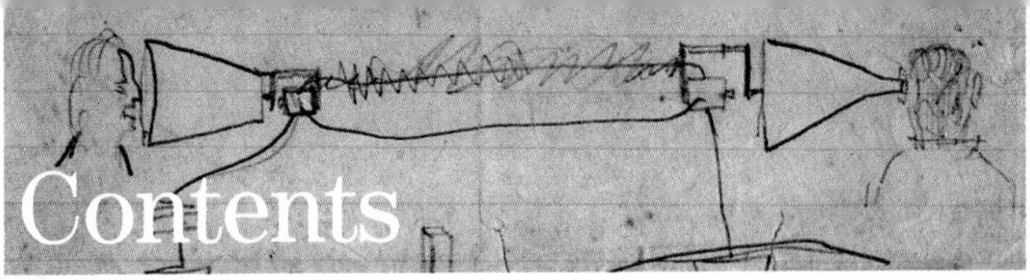

Contents

Introduction
Meet Alexander Graham Bell   7

Chapter 1
The Young Bell   9

Chapter 2
Teaching Speech   15

Chapter 3
Racing to Be First   19

Chapter 4
Making the Telephone   25

Chapter 5
Other Inventions   31

Report Guide   36

Glossary   38

Further Reading   39

Index   40

Alexander Graham Bell made the first telephone call from New York to Chicago in 1892.

Meet Alexander Graham Bell

Alexander Graham Bell grew up in a family that had a special interest in teaching deaf people to speak. Both his father and his grandfather were speech teachers. Alexander became a teacher of the deaf, too.

Alexander Graham Bell was also an inventor. He was curious about the world around him. He was always exploring and making new discoveries. He taught during the day and experimented at night.

Alexander Graham Bell's most famous invention was the telephone. This "talking machine" forever changed the way people communicate.

Bell's mother, Eliza Symonds Bell, was a painter and a musician who loved to play the piano. She used the ear tube she is holding to hear the music.

Chapter 1

The Young Bell

Alexander Graham Bell was born in
Edinburgh, Scotland, on March 3, 1847. He
was the second of three sons. Alexander was
named for his grandfather, Alexander Bell.
At the age of 11, he gave himself a middle
name, Graham.

Bell's mother was almost deaf and used
an ear tube to help her hear. She sometimes
used sign language to communicate with her
children. With sign language, people can
"talk" with their hands. They make special
movements with their fingers to form letters
and words.

Even though she had a hearing problem, Bell's mother was a fine musician. She put her ear tube on the soundboard of the piano. This way she could hear the notes by feeling the vibrations the piano made.

Think about this. If you cannot hear, then how can you speak? You don't know how to make sounds. Bell's father had invented a way to teach deaf people to speak. It was called the "Visible Speech" system.

In his teens, Alexander Graham Bell enjoyed music, photography, and exploring nature.

Alexander Graham Bell uses Visible Speech symbols to teach a student how to talk.

Bell had created symbols that spelled out words. Each symbol showed how to use your tongue and lips to make certain sounds. The different symbols showed deaf people how to pronounce words they could not hear.

The Bell family relaxes in their garden at Milton Cottage, near Edinburgh, Scotland. (left to right): Melville, Alexander, Mrs. Bell, Edward, and Mr. Bell.

Bell took after his father and started inventing when he was a boy. His father's friend, a mill owner, invited him to create something useful. And he did. Bell created a tool to take the husks, or outer shells, off wheat kernels. He did not become rich or famous from his first invention. But he learned that he could invent things. He and his brother built a speaking machine that could say "Mama."

Young Bell may have been very smart, but he was not a good student. He had no interest in Greek or Latin, two important subjects taught at school. Instead, he wanted to study plants and animals. Like his mother, he loved music and took piano lessons.

After Bell graduated from high school, his father sent him to live and study with his grandfather in London, England. Bell's grandfather was a speech expert. He taught people how to be better speakers. At that time, people had to talk loudly and clearly to be heard. There were no microphones or public address systems as there are today.

Bell enjoyed living with his grandfather. His grandfather let Bell make his own decisions. Young Bell became a more serious student. He learned a lot about the human voice and how it works. He decided that he would become a teacher like his grandfather and father.

Young Alexander (called Alec) poses with his grandfather, Alexander Bell, and his father, Alexander Melville Bell (called Melville).

As a young man, Alexander Graham Bell was a successful teacher of the deaf and a speech professor at Boston University.

Chapter 2

Teaching Speech

Bell applied for a job as a teacher of speech and music in Scotland. Although he was only 16 years old, he got the job. Some of his students were older than he was. While teaching, Bell studied the human voice. He also experimented with sound.

Bell's family moved to London. There, his father taught his system of Visible Speech. Bell joined his family in London. He began teaching his father's system to children with hearing and speech problems. He took classes at the university and continued to test his ideas on sound and electricity.

Alexander Graham Bell (top right) poses with students and teachers at the Boston School for the Deaf where he taught.

Bell was sure that the human voice could travel through electrical wires.

Tragedy then struck the Bell family. Bell's two brothers died from tuberculosis, a disease that affects the lungs. Bell became ill, too, and his father feared that he would die. So, Bell's father moved the family to Canada. He thought Canada was a healthier place to live. Bell was 23 years old.

Bell became well again and soon wanted to live his own life. A year after moving to Canada, he moved to Boston, in the United States. A young woman, Sarah Fuller, had started a school in Boston using his father's speech system. Bell went there to teach.

Unlike many teachers at the time, Bell was patient with his students. He showed them how the voice worked. He taught them to use their fingers to feel their speech. He showed them how to move their lips and tongue to make sounds. Bell had great success with many of his students. Word spread and soon more parents began sending their children to the school where he taught.

At night, Bell experimented with sound waves and vibrations. He was looking for a way to use electricity to send vowel sounds through telegraph wires. These experiments with sound would lead to his invention of the telephone.

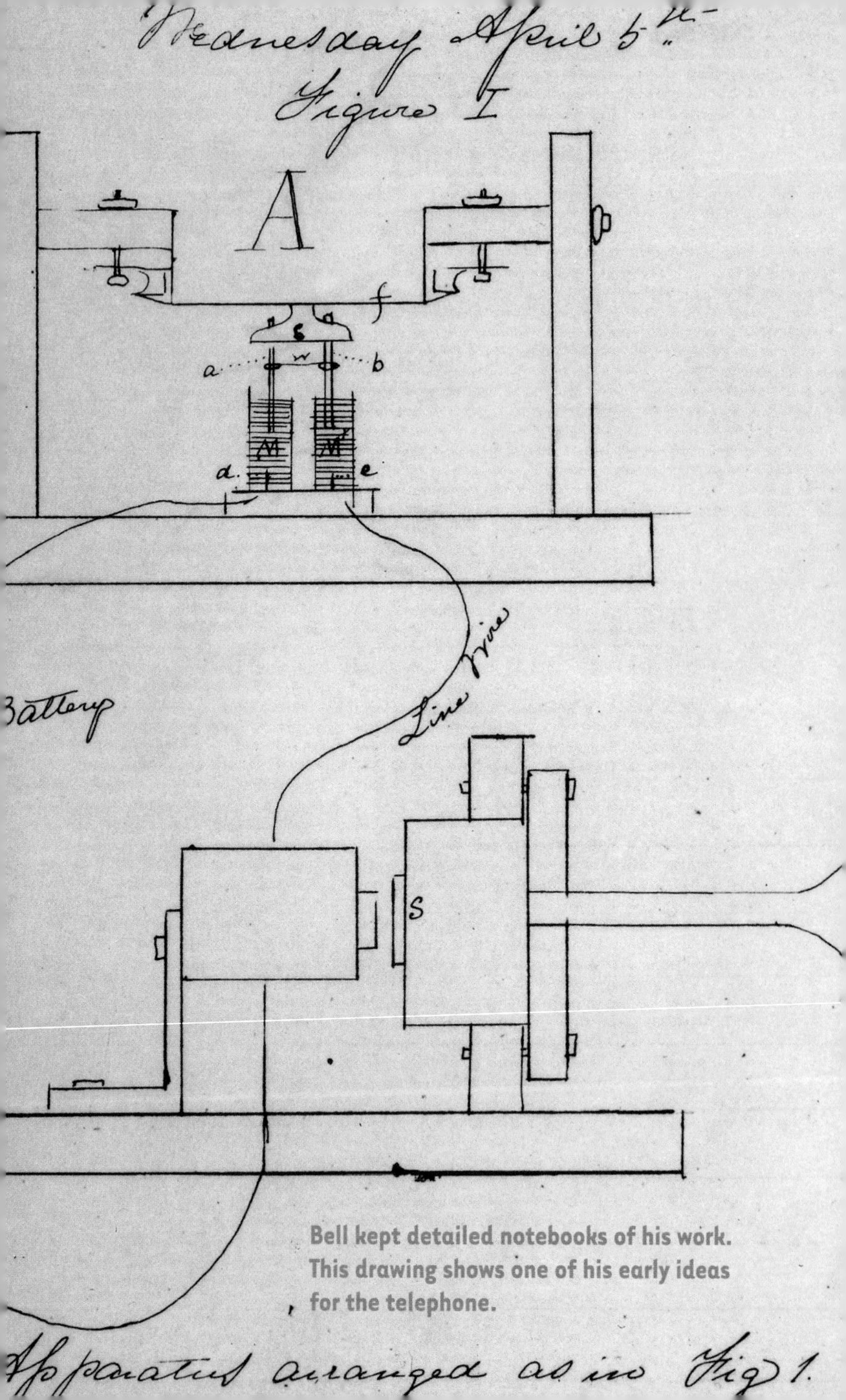

Wednesday April 5th

Figure I

A

f

s

a ... w ... b

d   e

Battery

Line Wire

S

Bell kept detailed notebooks of his work.
This drawing shows one of his early ideas
for the telephone.

Apparatus arranged as in Fig 1.

Chapter 3

Racing to Be First

Bell became a professor at a university in Boston. He also gave private lessons. One of his students was Mabel Hubbard. She had become deaf at the age of five from a disease called scarlet fever. They fell in love. They would marry two years later.

This photo of newlywed Mabel Hubbard Bell was taken during her honeymoon in England.

Bell experimented with the transmission of sound by electricity in this laboratory in Boston.

Mabel's father, Gardiner Hubbard, was a successful businessman and lawyer. Bell told Gardiner Hubbard and Thomas Sanders, the father of another of Bell's students, about his experiments and ideas. The two men liked what they heard. They knew Bell was determined and hardworking. So, they agreed to be his partners and give him money to work full-time on his ideas. This was important because other inventors were also working on ideas like Bell's. The first one to invent a machine to send messages over an electric wire would become rich.

A university loaned Bell a laboratory where he could work. Bell discussed his experiments with scientists he knew. He hired Thomas Watson as his assistant. Watson knew a lot about electricity. He could quickly build machines from sketches Bell had drawn. They made a good team.

Bell and Watson tried different ways to convert, or change, sound waves so that speech could be transmitted over telegraph wires. At the same time, another inventor, Elisha Gray, was working to complete a machine he had invented called a "speaking telegraph." It was a race to the United States Patent Office.

Thomas Watson first met Alexander Graham Bell while he was working in an electrical shop in Boston.

Bell experimented with many speaking machines
before he invented the telephone.

A patent is a paper from the government
that gives the holder certain rights. For a set
period of time, only the holder of the patent
can sell, use, or make a certain invention.
Whoever got the patent first would "own"
the invention of the telephone.

On June 2, 1875, Bell accidentally made a discovery about how and why a telephone might work. Quickly, he sketched a machine that he thought could send and receive sounds and had Watson build it. The machine was able to transmit sound, but it couldn't transmit the human voice. It couldn't transmit a conversation. More work had to be done.

Bell worked on his patent application for months. But Gardiner Hubbard couldn't wait. Wanting to be the first to file for the patent, Hubbard filed Bell's unfinished application on February 14, 1876. Just two hours later, Gray applied for a patent as well. Bell was awarded the patent. He had won the race by just two hours!

In his patent application, Bell had to swear that he was the inventor and planned to become an American citizen.

Chapter 4

Making the Telephone

Now, Bell had to actually make a telephone that worked. He and Watson continued to test different models. Finally, on March 10, 1876, Bell sent his voice over the wires!

Bell was in one room and Watson was in a different one. Bell said, "Mr. Watson, come here. I want you!" Watson rushed in saying that he had heard Bell's voice! Bell's voice was hard to hear, but it still seemed like a miracle.

◄ The invention of the telephone became a popular topic for artists to paint. This painting by American artist Dean Cornwell is titled "Alexander Graham Bell in His Laboratory."

Bell, right, shows Emperor Dom Pedro II of Brazil how to use a telephone receiver during the Centennial Exposition at Philadelphia.

Bell and Watson worked to make the sound of the human voice clearer and easier to understand. At first, speech traveled only one way. Bell worked on his telephone and put a transmitter and receiver at both ends of the phone. Then people could have two-way conversations, just like we can today.

The next step for Bell was to make people believe that the telephone was a useful invention. He wanted people to buy and use it. Some people thought the telephone was more like a toy.

In 1876, there was a big science and technology fair in Philadelphia. Many people showed their inventions. Scientists and businessmen visited the fair. Bell decided to show his invention, too. Once people heard Bell's voice come over the wire, the telephone became the hit of the fair. The judges at the fair gave him an award. Newspapers carried stories about this strange new device.

Bell, with Watson, Hubbard, and Sanders, formed the Bell Telephone Company. Bell left the selling and making of the telephone to his partners. He went off to London with his new wife, Mabel.

While Bell was in London, the telephone became famous. People asked Bell to show

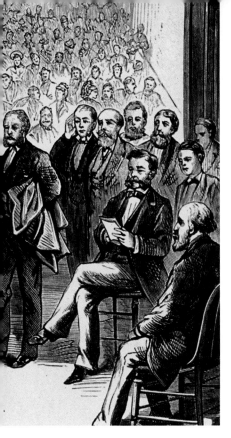

Alexander Graham Bell promoted his telephone through paid demonstrations. The first money he earned for inventing the telephone was $149 he was paid for a demonstration.

them how his invention worked. Queen Victoria, the ruler of Great Britain, asked Bell to show her how to use the telephone. She loved it. She demanded that phones be put in her palace. By 1880, the telephone had become one of the most famous and popular inventions of all time.

Until his death at the age of 75, Alexander Graham Bell continued to sketch his ideas and keep detailed lab notes of his experiments.

Chapter 5

Other Inventions

Alexander Graham Bell's invention made him a rich man. He decided that he did not want to be involved in business. He just wanted to be an inventor. So, Bell left the Telephone Company. He was only 32 years old.

In 1879, Bell and his family moved to Washington, D.C. There, he built a research laboratory and continued to invent. He kept notes on all his ideas and sketched his experiments. Not all Bell's experiments worked. Many failed, but that didn't stop him. He continued to explore. One discovery would lead to another.

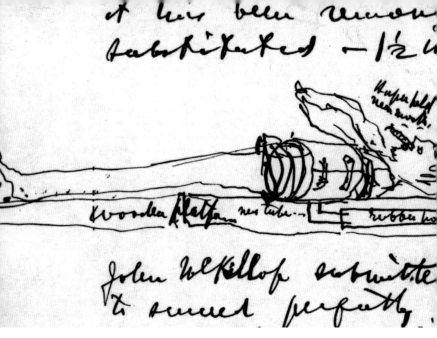

Bell sketched his ideas for a machine to help people breathe.

On July 2, 1881, President James A. Garfield was shot. One bullet entered his lower back, but doctors could not find it. In those days, there were no X-rays. So, the doctors asked Bell to invent something that could locate the bullet. After working for weeks, Bell invented two metal detectors, but neither one could save the president. However, one of the detectors was later used in military hospitals and helped save many lives.

Another machine Bell invented that has saved the lives of thousands of people is still being used today. It was invented in response to a sad event in his life. One of Bell's sons had died hours after being born because he had trouble breathing. Bell decided to invent a machine to help people breathe. His invention pumped air in and out of a person's lungs. It became the model for a machine known today as the "iron lung."

Bell (right) and his assistants fly a giant kite as his grandson runs under it. The kite, made up of pyramid-like triangles within a frame, was lightweight but very strong.

Bell loved to design and fly kites. He also experimented with airplane flight. He and his team designed and built the first plane with wing flaps for smoother takeoffs and landings.

Bell also built a boat that had skis. That boat is now known as a hydrofoil. In 1919, it set a world water-speed record.

Bell passed his love of learning to his children and grandchildren. He encouraged them "to think, to experiment, to try things on their own." He designed over 100 scientific experiments for them to do.

Alexander Graham Bell received many awards for his work. People all over the world knew and admired him. When Bell died, in 1922 at age 75, all the telephones in the United States were quiet for one minute. The American Telephone and Telegraph Company (AT&T) did this to honor Bell.

Alexander Graham Bell invented the graphophone, a phonograph that played wax records.

How to Write an A+ Report

1. Choose a topic.

- Find something that interests you.
- Make sure it is not too big or too small.

2. Find sources.

- Ask your librarian for help.
- Use many different sources: books, magazine articles, and Web sites.

3. Gather information.

- Take notes. Write down the big ideas and interesting details.
- Use your own words.

4. Organize information.

- Sort your notes into groups that make sense.

- Make an outline. Put your groups of notes in the order you want to write your report.

5. Write your report.

- Write an introduction that tells what the report is about.

- Use your outline and notes as you write to make sure you say everything you want to say in the order you want to say it.

- Write an ending that tells about your report.

- Write a title.

6. Revise and edit your report.

- Read your report to make sure it makes sense.

- Read it again to check spelling, punctuation, and grammar.

7. Hand in your report!

Glossary

hydrofoil   a boat with underwater foils or fins that travels above the water surface at high speeds

patent   the right given by the government to an inventor to be the only one making or selling the invention for a set period of time

receiver   the part of the telephone you speak into

scarlet fever   a contagious disease causing a high fever and bright-red (scarlet) skin

sign language   a way of talking by using hand movements to form letters and words

sound waves   the vibrations that carry sound through the air

technology   the use of tools and ideas to solve problems and make life better for people

transmitter   a device that sends out a signal from one place to another

tuberculosis   a disease of the lungs

vibrations   the rapid back and forth movements of an object that produces sounds

Further Reading

• Books •

Haven, Kendall. *Alexander Graham Bell: Inventor and Visionary* (Great Life Stories). New York: Franklin Watts, 2003. Grades 5 & Up, 128 pages.

Matthews, Tom L. *Always Inventing: Alexander Graham Bell.* Washington, D.C.: National Geographic Society, 1999. Grades 5 & Up, 64 pages.

Pollard, Michael. *Giants of Science–Alexander Graham Bell.* Farmington Hills, MI: Blackbirch Press, 2000. Grades 3–5, 64 pages.

Sherrow, Victoria. *Alexander Graham Bell* (On My Own Biography). Minneapolis, MN: Carolrhoda Books, 2001. Grades 1–3, 48 pages.

Webster, Christine. *Alexander Graham Bell and the Telephone* (Cornerstones of Freedom Second Series). New York: Children's Press, 2004. Grades 3–6, 48 pages.

• Web Sites •

Alexander Graham Bell Institute
http://bell.uccb.ns.ca/

Alexander Graham Bell Association for the Deaf and Hard of Hearing
http://www.agbell.org/

American Telephone & Telegraph Coporation (AT&T)
http://www.corp.att.com/history

Library of Congress American Memory
www.memory.loc.gov/ammem/bellhtml/bellhome.html

PBS American Experience
www.pbs.org/wgbh/amex/telephone/peopleevents/mabell.html

Index

Bell, Alexander Graham
    inventor 9, 11, 12, 17, 20–21, 23, 25–26, 31, 32–33
    student 12–13
    teacher 14, 15, 16, 17, 19, 34
Bell, Alexander (grandfather) . 7, 9, 13
Bell, Eliza Symonds (mother) . 8, 10, 12
Bell, Melville (father) 7, 10–11, 13, 16
Bell Telephone Company 28, 31
Centennial Exposition 26, 27
Gray, Elisha 21, 23
Hubbard, Gardiner 20, 23, 28
Hubbard, Mabel 19, 28
inventions
    hydrofoil 34
    iron lung 33
    kites 34
    telephone 17, 18, 21, 23, 25, 27
patents 21–22, 23
Sanders, Thomas 20, 28
sign language 9
Visible Speech 10–11, 15
Watson, Thomas 21, 23, 25, 27, 28

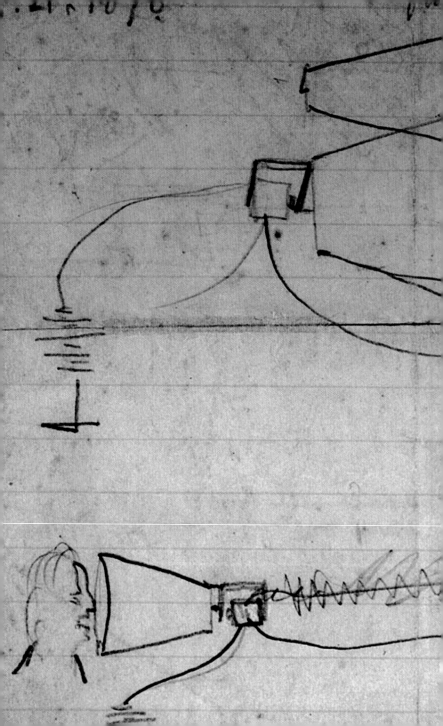